Beautiful
PRESENTS

The Creative Craft of Gift Wrapping

Text and Package Designs
by Richard Kollath

Photographs by Tony Cenicola

Running Press Book Publishers
Philadelphia, Pennsylvania

International representatives: Worldwide Media Services Inc., 115 East Twenty-third Street, New York, NY 10010.

9 8 7 6 5 4 3 2 1

Digit on the right indicates the number of this printing.

Library of Congress Cataloging-in-Publication Number

87-042628

ISBN 0-89471-559-3

Typeset by Lettering Directions
Printed and bound in Hong Kong

This book may be ordered from the publisher.
Please include $1.50 postage.
But try your bookstore first.

Running Press Book Publishers
125 South 22nd Street
Philadelphia, Pennsylvania 19103

DEDICATION

For Ruth, John, Teri, and Jason, with love.

ACKNOWLEDGMENTS

My appreciation and thanks to Harry Dennis, Barbara Miller of Hallmark Cards, Inc., Susan Rosenthal of The Stephen Lawrence Co., Ed Gilles and Alan Smith of Contempo, Donna Lichtenstein of Fiber Craft, Elli Schneider of Offray Ribbons, Bill Miller of Ribbon Narrow, Sonnie Levin of Balloon City, USA, and Carolyn and Stephen Waligurski of Hurley Patentee Manor for their generosity and kind support.

CONTENTS

Chapter One

BASICS

There are many creative ways to wrap a package so it reflects the personal thoughtfulness of the giver—the extra care and attention that went into choosing the gift in the first place. There is a special satisfaction in giving a gorgeously wrapped gift, and yet it is extremely easy to do. You need to have only a few basic materials on hand and to understand a few elementary techniques to wrap the types of packages that will draw "oohs" and "ahs" before they are even opened.

The necessary supplies are a good sharp pair of ribbon-and-paper scissors, an extra roll or two of double-faced tape, standard transparent tape, a selection of ribbons and papers, a desk stapler, a kitchen knife, a pen that works for writing just the right note to accompany your package, and an assortment of yarns, gift tags, and small objects that are easy to attach to the package top and relay the message, "I have taken extra care in giving you this gift." Take advantage of sales and keep some surprises in your supply chest; a few sachets of potpourri, an ornament or two, strands of costume jewelry, children's books, small toys, coloring pencils, or crayons will find their way into good use.

Mastering a few basic techniques will enable you to achieve the look you wish to have for your package and free you from some common frustrations at the same time. It is a good idea to practice a bit before wrapping your first real gift, keeping in mind that your goal is to finish up with a crisp, elegantly tailored box that has smooth surfaces, clearly defined corners, and neatly tied bows. All the components should come across as well thought out and well executed.

The Basic Seamless Wrap is just what it sounds like—an easy way of wrapping your packages so that they look smooth and professional.

1. To begin, take a standard shirt box and, using the diagram as a guide, mark the sides of your box with the letter identifications, A through F.

2. Having selected your paper, lay it out right side down and place side A of the box upon it. Make sure you have sufficient paper to cover the whole box, then add an additional 3 inches (7½ centimeters) and cut off any excess paper.

3. With side A face down upon the paper, draw up one long end of the paper over sides F, B, and D, having 1 inch (2½ centimeters) of overlap to

secure on side A. Tape along the paper edge to secure.

4. Bring the remaining long end of the paper up over side A to the junction of A and D. Mark where the edge of the box meets the paper.

5. Fold the remaining paper under so that the paper edge lines up exactly with the edge where sides A and D meet. Run a length of double-faced tape along the length of the box along side A, and press down the paper. A continuous seamless piece of paper should now surround your box, with its ends remaining open.

6. To secure the ends, you may have to trim the paper. If so, trim each end to the approximate width of sides C and E

plus about another inch (2½ centimeters).

7. Fold down the end from side C so
that two triangles of paper stick out on
each side. Crease their edges and fold
them inward. Bring the bottom side, B,
up to the top of side A and measure the
overlap. Mark it and fold it to meet with
the top edge of A. Again, run double-
faced tape the length of the edge of side
B so that it will secure the paper. Now
you should have a precise edge that
meets flush to the top of the package,
and it is at this point that you may have
to make a subtle adjustment in your
fold so that the end of your box retains a
crispness.

8. Repeat the same process on side E.

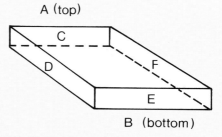

The illustration shows a rectangular
box with standard proportions. If you
find your box has higher sides, remember to trim some of the paper off when
wrapping the ends so that the paper lies
flat and free of wrinkles.

The Seamless Wrap is easy to master
and will serve as the base for many creative departures. It takes a little practice
but is a very simple way of making a gift
box look its tailored best.

Another basic and traditional way of wrapping a gift box is with the Keepsake Wrap. With this method, the paper does not form a seamless shell around the box. Instead, you wrap the bottom and top of the box separately so that it may be reused. The box itself now becomes another gift, and the possibilities in wrapping it are endless. It can be covered in paper, fabric, or even sheet moss and dried flowers. The process is very similar to that of the Basic Seamless Wrap. There are several differences, however.

1. To begin, place the bottom half of a rectangular box on your paper, which is face down on the working surface.

2. Pull up enough paper to cover both of the short end sides of the box and allow enough paper to overlap into the inside of the box by 1½ inches (4 centimeters).

3. Cut the paper and bring up both sides. Lightly tape to secure the ends to the inside of the box, but only as a temporary measure.

4. Repeat the trimming and folding of the ends, keeping enough paper to overlap the top edge with the same proportion as the side. Tape lightly to secure and repeat with the other end.

5. When all the sides have been pulled into the interior of the box, you may make any adjustments in smoothing and tightening the sides of the paper. After this has been done, use invisible tape to secure the paper to the box surface.

6. Repeat this whole process to wrap the top of the box. What you should end up with is a wrapped box with a removable top.

Beautiful combinations of papers can be used with dramatic effects. Don't be afraid to mix patterns, colors, and designs of different proportions. Fabric is also a perfect material with which to create a keepsake box. The wrapping procedure is similar to that when using paper, but instead of securing the fabric with tape, use white glue (it doesn't matter what kind). The tackier the glue, the quicker the fabric adheres to the box. Some manufacturers of white glue make a specific product for fabric. Simply glue the ends of the fabric the same way you secured the paper with tape. While this will hold most fabric, you may want to cover the entire box surface with glue; this will bind the fabric to the box like an extra skin and make the package nearly indestructible. The hat box on page 34 and the covered boxes on pages 40 and 41 were all created by adhering the fabric to the box in the latter way.

By having a command of the Basic Seamless Wrap as well as the process for creating the Keepsake Wrap, you will be in control of the essentials needed to adapt your creative ideas into package realities.

Chapter Two

PAPER

One of the varied components that can make an ordinary package extraordinary is the use of paper. In this chapter let's believe that everything is possible and that the combinations of the enormous array of materials make the boundaries of wrapping limitless. The wrapping papers available today (both in packages and rolls) are so versatile they can be used alone or combined with other papers to create a personal statement. Using solid colors in combination with patterns, or stripes with dots, or simply taking little shapes cut or torn from one color paper and gluing them against a background of another color, can fulfill your creative desires.

You'll find that paper that is not intentionally designed for gift wrapping can also be put to use. Choose newspaper in a foreign language, shelf paper, wallpaper, Japanese rice paper, tissue, cellophane, or simple brown wrapping paper. Consider everything as a vehicle for your talents.

These three cylinders waiting to go to a party are dressed up in colored tissue. Over the tissue, a piece of opalescent cellophane adds a slightly mysterious festive covering. Each end is tied with cording complementary to the colors of the tissue, and the three cylinders are then neatly attached with a basic bow of opalescent ribbon. You can change the colors of this wrap for specific occasions or even seasons. Autumn rusts and ochers, spring pastels, hot and vivid summer brights, or cooling winter tints of tissue make this wrapping an anytime possibility. Adding stickers or cut-out shapes from flower catalogs, or having children draw on the tissue or the underside of the cellophane with magic markers, will give your package a special look.

You can create your own patterned paper by sponge painting, a perfect family activity, especially during holiday preparations. All you need is a few rolls of wrapping paper, a pen, some clean kitchen sponges, sharp scissors, acrylic paint, and a shallow dish or pie plate, and you're ready to have fun. This technique is so versatile that you can cover an entire box with sponged shapes, or use it to enhance plain or prepatterned paper.

1. Cover a work surface with some newspaper.

2. Next, use a pen to draw the outline of whatever shapes you wish to reproduce on the sponges, then cut them out using sharp scissors.

3. Pour the paint into the pie plate or dish.

4. Simply dip the sponge into the paint, then press it upon the package. One word of caution: if the sponge has too much paint on it, it will leave a blurred image. To control the amount of paint, dip the sponge into the paint and then test it on a paper towel or newspaper. Use acrylic paint, as it dries rapidly. Best of all, it's easy to clean up with only water.

Stenciling is another great way to personalize a package. To stencil paper, you need a few extra tools: a sharp art knife (such as an X-acto), stencil paints (available in kits or individual containers), a stencil brush (one with stiff bristles), and stencil paper (heavy typing paper can be substituted). All supplies are inexpensive and available through catalogs, or at art-supply or crafts stores. Precut stencil designs and stencil books in a variety of shapes, including the alphabet, are available so that you need not actually draw the design—unless, of course, you want to. Hand-cut stencils by tracing any number of images, even a child's drawing.

1. After selecting your design, trace it upon the stencil paper.

2. With the art knife, cut through the stencil paper (always use cardboard underneath to protect your work surface) until you have a hole in the shape you want to stencil on the package.

3. Mix your paint and place the stencil paper on your already-wrapped package.

4. Dip the stenciling brush into the paint and gently but firmly dab the cut-out area of the stencil shape until you have totally colored in the hole in the stencil paper.

This bright and happy gift box has been cheerfully decorated with hearts torn from a solid-colored giftwrap paper and glued onto the yellow package. Tearing is great fun, and you can never make a mistake, simply an unexpected abstract shape. Gluing one shape upon another adds dimension and texture to your package. Combining pure colors with torn pictures or shapes from patterned papers also adds to the richness. However energetic you wish to become, experiment and make paper designing part of your wrapping repertoire, and your presents will never look the same again.

1. To tear the colored paper and expose the white edge, tear the whole shape around in one direction.

2. Then simply glue the hearts onto your package with a thin, even layer of white glue.

5. If you need to add paint, remember the suggestions given with sponging. Dab the paint-laden brush onto a paper towel first so that you retain control over the amount of paint.

6. Allow the paint to dry before removing the stencil; otherwise, you chance smearing your design.

7. Repeat the process until you have covered as much of the paper as desired.

Chapter Three

RIBBON

Just as there are many wonderful things to be done with paper, ribbon also extends the potential for delightful package creations. Fortunately, there are a multitude of possibilities to select from. Ribbon runs the gamut from kitchen twine to self-stick coordinating prepackaged bows, double-faced satin, grosgrains, tapestry ribbons, cording, and curling ribbons. Ribbon is the essential complement to gift paper and can bring it beautifully alive.

When choosing ribbon, it is important to select a color and width that is appropriate to the scale of the package, as well as the coloration of the paper. It is not essential to match the ribbon with the paper in a monochromatic way. You should feel free to be expressive with color, which is half the fun and part of the creative process. But, in truth, you also should not shock with grossly improper color or pattern selection. A good rule is to select a color from the pattern of the paper you are using, or ribbon that is in the same family of color as the paper. To cross over to a complementary color can be dangerous if the

colors together become visually jarring. Many papers have ribbons that come preselected. You may choose to follow those combinations or to explore independently.

Perhaps the most essential advice is to tie up your gift with the same attention to detail that you applied to the wrapping. Always keep in mind the scale of your package and the bows or ornaments you attach to it. Is the bow too large for the package? Is the print of the paper in keeping with the proportions of the box? In the end, you must rely upon your own instincts and taste, as in all creative expressions. But you should never lose awareness of the importance of scale, or your presents will have an unbalanced look to them.

Using a standard shirt box as a measure, you will need about two and a half yards (two meters) of ribbon to tie up the average package and make a full basic bow. A larger or smaller package will require either more or less ribbon. Tying up your package and creating the basic bow is described on the next page.

1. Do not precut your ribbon. Several too-short pieces will lead to immediate frustration. Simply lay out a length of ribbon and place your gift package face down upon it.

2. Bring up the ends of the ribbon to the center of the box and form a twist.

3. Holding the ribbon tightly, turn both the ribbon and the box over so that you are now looking at the top of your gift and you have two ends of ribbon in your hands.

4. Bring the ends together, and be sure you will have enough ribbon to make a simple knot and a bow with sufficient ends. If not, make the adjustment from the back side.

5. Using the same method as tying your shoe strings, simply take the two ends of ribbon and secure a simple knot and loop bow with long, flowing ends.

Three lengths of cranberry-colored grosgrain ribbon were tied separately around this gift enhanced with marbleized paper. A subtle flourish has

been created by simply altering the positions of the bows, giving the wrapping a visual energy. In addition, the monochromatic paper and ribbon har-monize well. To change the character of this ribbon treatment, simply use rib-bons of different widths or colors—or perhaps some with patterns or stripes.

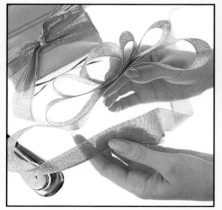

The two-loop bow has a straightforward simplicity that is both stylish and elegant. The delight of bow making, however, comes with the variations possible with multiple-loop bows in various ribbons. To create a multiple-loop bow and tie up your package, you will need between five and a half and six yards (between five and five and a half meters) of ribbon.

1. Tie a length of ribbon around the width of a wrapped package and tie a knot with plenty of excess ribbon at the end.

2. Using the same color ribbon, start at one end and make a small loop. Hold the loop together between the thumb and forefinger of one hand. Do not cut the ribbon.

3. Still holding the loop together, make a second slightly larger loop underneath the first, and slip it between the same two fingers.

4. Make three additional loops (or more) using the same method (as shown in the photo), slipping each between your fingers to hold the bow tightly. Cut the ribbon.

5. Carefully moving your fingers to one side, staple the bow together in the center, underneath the top of the first loop as shown in the photo. Staple through all the other loops.

6. Tie the bow to the package through the center loop, using the ends of the ribbon already on the package.

You can add an extra special touch to even the most basic bow by using curling ribbon, which is great fun to work with. Children love it since there is the extra excitement of actually curling the long ends once the bow has been made. Following the basic bow-making process, simply allow a number of extra inches to trail from the bow at the ends of the ribbon. Once the bow has been secured to the package, hold the ribbon between your thumb and the sharp edge of your opened scissors or kitchen knife. Pull the sharp edge of your scissors or a kitchen knife. Holding the instrument in your hand, pull its edge along the length of ribbon. When released, the ribbon should pop into a bouncing ringlet. Continue the process until every length of ribbon has its own curl. The length of the ribbon will determine the playfulness of the spirit of the bow and the overall look of the package. Curling ribbon has an uplifting feel about it, and the available colors are rich and varied.

Although this festive wreath with its metallic premade bows and gold leaves says, "Christmas," the same idea can be adapted to any occasion by using colors and materials echoing other seasons. To make this wreath, however, take some gilded leaves (available at crafts or florist shops) and, using a thin layer of white glue, attach them in a circle on top of a package that's been wrapped in red paper with the Basic Seamless Wrap method. Then simply peel off the protective tape from several premade bows and stick them onto the wreath of leaves, alternating the colors to form a pattern. (For a twist on the traditional, you may want to present the package as a diamond shape.)

This bouquet of tissue paper flowers is a beautiful yet easily constructed addition to your gift. You will need the following supplies: several sheets of brightly colored tissue paper, cut into 60 four-inch (ten-centimeter) squares, 20 three-inch (eight-centimeter) wooden picks with wire (available at florists or crafts shops), and a half dome of styrofoam (around three inches—or eight centimeters—in diameter) with a self-stick adhesive pad on the flat side. This is also widely available at either florists or crafts shops. Keep in mind that these instructions only sound complicated. After you've completed your first flower, you'll realize just how easy the whole process is.

1. Fold 1 square of tissue into quarters. Then, starting at the end opposite the fold, cut a heart-shaped "petal" from the tissue paper. Take care, however, not to cut all the way through the folded edge or your "flower" will come apart.

2. Unfold the tissue to release the flowers. Then, taking 3 flowers at a time, each of a different color, twist them together lightly from their centers so that the petals turn upwards and the flowers take their shape.

3. Next, lay the group of flowers against a wooden pick and wrap the wire from the pick around the flowers to bind them together. Repeat steps 2 and 3 until all the flowers have been twisted around the wooden picks.

4. Stick the picks into the half dome of styrofoam, spacing them evenly around the dome. Then peel off the covering from the self-adhesive strip, and place your creation on the top of your wrapped gift.

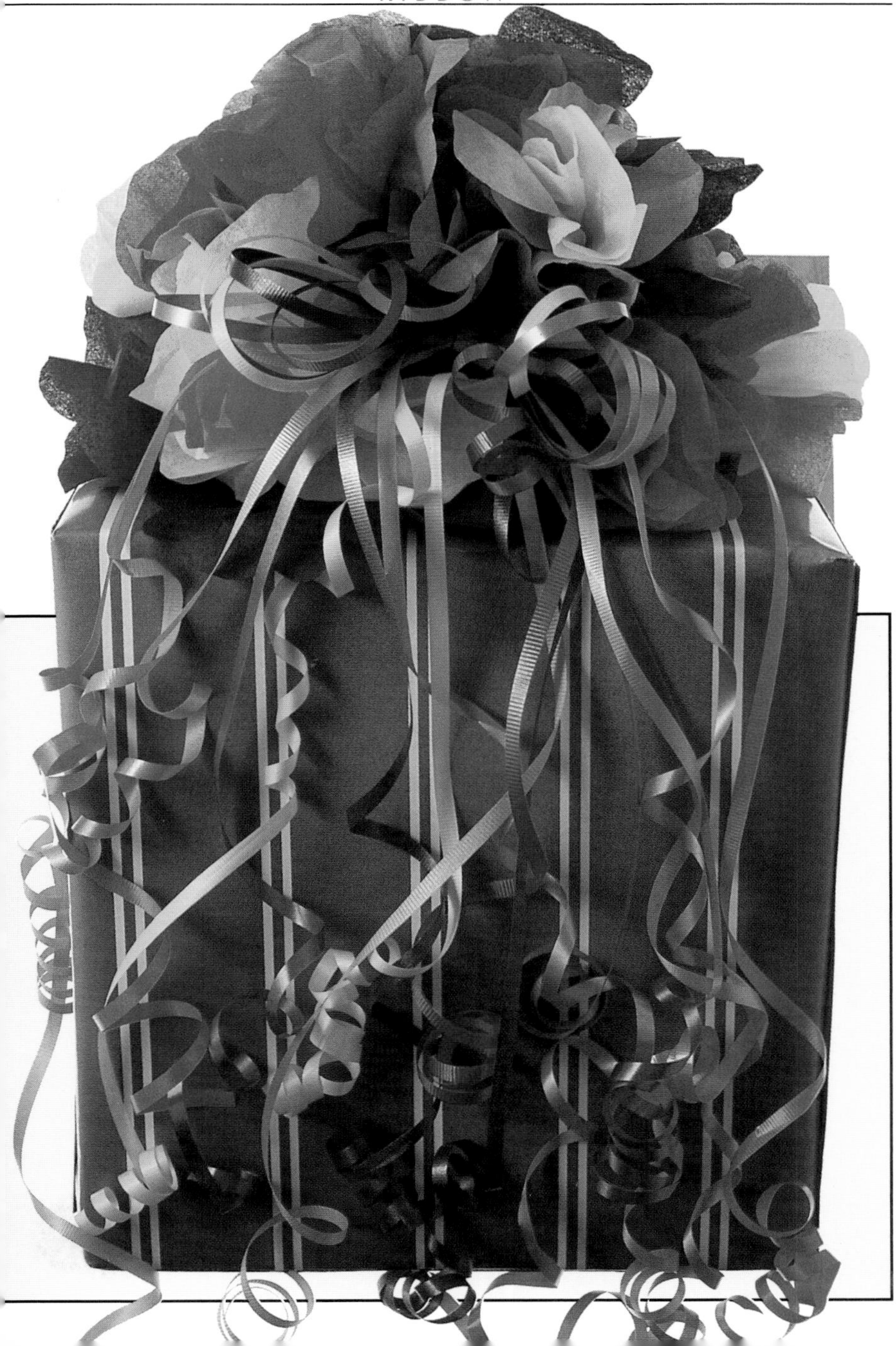

Chapter Four

THEMES AND OCCASIONS

Birthdays, holidays, and times of special achievement are occasions for a gift that really means something. Now your gift wrapping can also carry special meaning. By selecting a decorating technique that follows a particular theme, you can create a package that matches the personality of the receiver and pays homage to it. In this way, the wrapping can become a gift in itself.

For the newborn or very young infant, a gift wrap reflecting the tender aspect of "babyhood" is best expressed through the choice of pastel papers, ribbons, and patterns, or the kind of personal treatment applied to the package in the photo. Soft pastel blue paper with torn hearts of a contrasting blue provides all the baby-boyness this gift needs. The full-looped bow of pastel stripes and the little yellow duck accentuate this theme.

The spirit of giving is multiplied with this wrapping, which sports two gifts on the outside of the box alone! Any young girl with a busy life would welcome a gift wrapped so that the top of the brightly papered box is a real blackboard that she can hang up and keep important information on. To create a board like the one in the photo, paint the frame of the blackboard using the sponging method discussed on page 14. Then, instead of attaching a card, you can write her name and a special greeting on a miniature blackboard that has also been sponge painted. This second blackboard will be perfect for her to use when playing with her dolls, or to keep in a book bag. Secure the blackboard with a deep orange ribbon, and don't forget to include some chalk!

that will cover the entire length of the tube and fit around its circumference. Wrap the paper around the tube and attach it using double-faced tape on the inside of the paper.

2. Cap the rocket with a red cone by folding a piece of red wrapping paper in half lengthwise with the red side out. Roll that piece of paper into a cone shape and tape the edges together on the inside with double-faced tape.

3. Carefully make about ten ½-inch long (1-centimeter long) vertical slits around the entire edge of the cone.

4. Being careful not to dent the cone, place it on top of the tube. It should extend about a ½ inch (1 centimeter) over the tube. Press the cut edge flush against the tube and tape it down.

5. To cover the tape and add an interesting detail, take the strip of paper, fold down any rough edges, and use double-faced tape to secure it to the place where the cone and tube meet on the inside of the strip.

6. Give the rocket blast-off reality by cutting two fins from cardboard and covering them with the red paper. Attach them to the tube with pieces of transparent or colored tape. That way the tape becomes part of the total design of the package while providing the necessary bonding of the fins to the rocket body.

Bright, spirited colors and patterns echo the energies of young children and enhance the presentation of gifts you are giving to them. For example, a young child will love the toy rocket surprise on this wrapping. For this wrap you will need an 8 - by - 15 - inch (28-by-38 centimeter) piece of paper with a large checked pattern, a 14-inch (36-centimeter) square of red wrapping paper, a strip of paper with a contrasting, smaller checked pattern, a round oatmeal box or similar large cardboard tube, some small scraps of cardboard · for the fins, glue, and double-faced tape.

1. To construct the rocket, cut a piece of paper with the larger checked pattern

When wrapping gifts for adults, it's often fun to create a theme that plays off of specific interests and hobbies. For an outdoorsman, for example, you can use a piece of camouflage fabric to wrap a box. For a wrap like the one in the photo, you will need a piece of camouflage fabric, double-faced tape, a length of raffia or twine, and a wooden or plastic bird (or other such ornament), available at crafts stores.

1. Following the instructions for the Basic Seamless Wrap on page 8, cover your box with the camouflage fabric.

2. To carry the theme further, wind raffia or twine around the box several times and tie a knot.

3. To top it all off, create a raffia pompon by simply wrapping the raffia around a 2-by-6-inch (5-by-15-centimeter) cardboard rectangle about 50 times, or until you reach your desired thickness. Use one hand to hold the raffia in place, and with the other slip it off the cardboard. Tie it securely in the center. Then cut the ends and—"poof!"—the pompon will explode into a rounded shape. Attach it to your package directly over the knot with double-faced tape, or a light, even layer of white glue.

4. Finally, tie any additional ornaments on for embellishment.

Other examples of theme packages include one wrapped in shiny blue paper and tied with nautical knots for the sailor. Or wrap the executive's gift with sheets of computer printout, graph paper for the accountant, maps and trip brochures for the traveler, or real estate listings for the realtor. Almost every job, hobby, or interest has some theme you can pick up on when wrapping. Anything you cannot buy, you can usually make in order to tailor your gift to a certain personality. Your imagination is your only limitation.

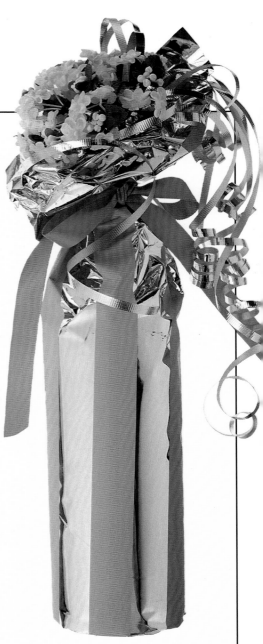

It is as easy to wrap up a bottle as it is to pop it into a brown bag, but it's so much nicer to receive it all dressed up. The paper and ribbon used will determine the overall look of the gift. If you wrap the bottle in metallic striped paper, its obvious counterpart is a metallic curling ribbon. Tying on extras such as silk or real flowers, noisemakers, balloons, or a sprig of holly will add to the charm of the wrap itself.

1. Take a length of gift paper and lay it face down on a flat surface.

2. Place the bottle against one edge of the paper, about 1 inch (2½ centimeters) from the bottom.

3. Secure the edge to the bottle with a tiny piece of tape, on the glass, not the label.

4. Roll it up. You will have a cylinder with more paper on the top of the bottle than at the base.

5. Clip the paper 1 inch (2½ centimeters) past the overlap and secure it on the inside with double-faced tape.

6. Then fold the bottom edges under, and tape them together, forming a closed surface.

7. Tie a basic bow at the neck of the bottle with a complementary-color ribbon, and allow the top of the paper to ripple up like a great collar. Use the technique described on page 24 to achieve long curls of ribbon.

This keepsake hat box has been covered in cotton chintz and tied together with a beautiful wide length of satin ribbon. The permanent covering of the box makes it a gift in itself, one that will be reused and remembered. In order to cover a box like this with fabric, you will need white glue, a small, stiff paintbrush, a pair of fabric scissors, and about a yard (one meter) of fabric for a 16- to 18-inch (40- to 45-centimeter) hat box.

1. Working with the bottom half of the box first, measure the height of its sides and add on an extra 2 inches (5 centimeters). This is how long your fabric should be.

2. Measure the circumference of the box, add on an inch (2½ centimeters), and that's how wide your fabric should

be. Now cut your fabric to size.

3. Working with a 6-inch (15-centimeter) square (or smaller) area at a time, brush white glue thinly and evenly on the sides of the bottom half.

4. Then, making sure the fabric is straight, lay it against the glued area, leaving 1 inch (2½ centimeters) hanging over both the lip and the bottom edges of the box, and not touching the glue. Press the fabric to the box firmly.

5. Flip the unattached fabric back to keep it off the glue, and brush glue on another 6-inch (15-centimeter) area next to the first one. Pull the fabric tight and press it down on that area, and continue to do so until all sides of the bottom half of the box have been covered.

6. At this point you should have about an inch (2½ centimeters) of extra fabric; fold it in half to make a hem, then overlap it with the other end and glue it down.

7. Next, fold over the extra inch (2½ centimeters) of fabric around the lip of the bottom half of the box and glue it down inside.

8. Fold over the extra inch (2½ centimeters) of fabric hanging over the bottom edge and glue it down on the underside of the box.

9. To cover the top half of the box, lay it down on the wrong side of the material and trace its outline. Add at least an inch (2½ centimeters) all the way around, and then cut it out.

10. Brush the lid of the box evenly with glue. Center the fabric on the lid and smooth it free of wrinkles.

11. Next, as shown in the photo, make slices in the fabric overhanging the lid so that it will lay flat against the sides of the lid. Glue it down.

12. Cut a long strip of material to cover that sliced fabric around the sides of the lid. This band should be wide enough so that there is enough fabric to turn both the top and bottom edges under. Turn the edges under and glue the material down to finish the lid.

Despite the number of steps involved, this process really takes very little time and produces a beautiful and lasting keepsake box. You can update the Victorian look of the one in the photo by using brighter, bolder colors and designs to complement the contemporary apartment, while gold-, silver-, or cream-colored fabric is perfect for a bridal keepsake. Whatever fabric you choose, this is one gift wrap that may actually outlast the gift.

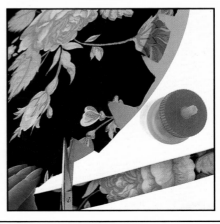

To depart from the traditional white, cream, gold, or silver colors commonly used for wrapping wedding gifts, try preparing a package with multiple layers of ties and papers. For this wrap, you will need a roll of solid aqua paper, a roll of handmade rice paper, scissors, double-faced tape, and equal-length pieces of pale aqua bridal tulle and satin cording (for a package the size of the one in the photo, you will need about two and a half yards—or two and a quarter meters—of each).

1. Using the Basic Seamless Wrap (see page 8), cover the box with solid aqua paper. Then using the Basic Seamless Wrap again, wrap over that with a piece of rice paper. The lace-like repetition of the rice paper's fan pattern allows the colored paper underneath to show through.

2. To tie it all up, lay the cording on the tulle, and following the instructions for basic bow tying on page 20, tie both together into a two-loop basic bow and let the ends trail romantically.

3. On the way to the celebration, buy (or pick) a rose to give this package the necessary color balance.

Flowers on packages? Of course. Pick them, buy them, or make them from tissue paper (see page 26). Used dried tussie-mussies (Victorian nosegays) or slip a single fresh blossom into the ribbon on a package.

Astack of boxes, each papered with the bright stripes of a wild zebra, become a whimsical departure for a festive gift presentation. Each box is of a different size, and a different color, but all are tied with a profusion of cascading ringlets from multicolored strands of curling ribbon (see page 24) that match the colors of the packages. To create papers like the ones in the photo requires hand painting. You can paint zebra stripes, or simply splatters, spots, or zigzags of bright colors.

Painting paper can become an activity the whole family can get involved in. All you need is some watercolor brushes, acrylic paints, a pie or muffin tin to hold the paints, an old rag to catch the spills, and a roll of plain white butcher's paper or drawing paper. Or

you can use special papers to produce a variety of effects. Rice paper will give your shapes and colors a softer edge, while a highly polished surface—like that of some wrapping papers—will produce a crisper image. The easiest paints to work with are acrylics. They dry quickly and are permanent, but wash off from your hands with water and a mild soap.

1. Spread your paper out on a large work surface and squeeze a small amount of paint from the tube into the tin.

2. Dip your brush in water, stir your paint, and you're ready to go.

3. Keep your brush in the water when you're contemplating what to do next, and clean it immediately after use.

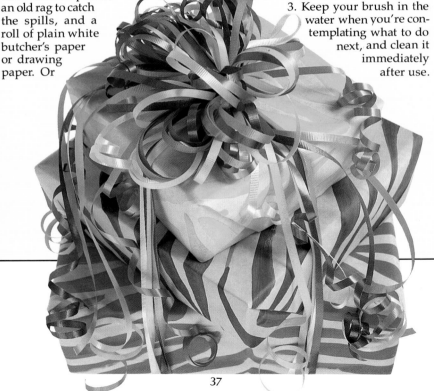

A small wooden heart-shaped box, which is available in most crafts stores, has been covered with moss to transform it into a poetic gift filled with sweet-scented potpourri—perfect for enclosing a piece of jewelry for a sweetheart. Although the heart shape may seem limited to Valentine's Day, it can be used throughout the year and treated in any number of thematic ways. Keep in mind that details are always important. Filling the heart with potpourri is one such loving touch. Adding just the thinnest satin ribbon enriches the visual combination of the moss and the dried flowers and lets the receiver know the care and attention that went into making this particular gift box.

To create this gift box, you'll need a small wooden heart-shaped box, a few large pieces of sheet moss (available from florists or crafts stores), some white glue, and a thin satin ribbon and some dried flowers, if you desire.

1. To begin, simply brush the top of the heart box evenly with glue and secure on top of it a piece of sheet moss large enough to cover the entire surface. Trim it around the edges by cutting with sharp scissors or by tearing it carefully.

2. Fit the top of the box back on the bottom, and draw a line around the circumference of the bottom half where it meets the top half.

3. Using that line as a guide, brush the bottom half of the box evenly with glue up to that line. Press a sheet of moss onto the glue, trim it to fit, and let both halves stand for at least an hour to dry.

4. If desired, you can fill the box with potpourri, add a few dried flowers to the top, and tie it up with a thin satin ribbon.

tree trim binds it all together, and a sprig of holiday greens adds a lovely fragrance and softness to the package.

1. Wrap the gift using the Basic Seamless Wrap, explained on page 8.

2. Next, tie it up with a length of gold-beaded tree trim, and tie it in a knot, letting the ends trail.

3. Tie a two-looped basic bow (see page 20) from wide red ribbon around the width of the package only, covering the knot of the tree trim but letting the rest of the gold beads show through.

4. Complete the wrap by garnishing it with some sprigs of ever-green tucked under the ribbons.

There are times during the year when a gift wrapped in a beautiful way can become an experience to be cherished. At Christmas there are certainly a harvest of gift-wrapping possibilities, with all the elaborate papers, ribbons, and decorative objects that are available. Often we are overwhelmed, unable to filter through the masses of potential. When you find a pleasing paper, ornament, or ribbon, it is a good idea to either buy it right then or take good notes so you can come back for it later. It is also advisable to wrap some gifts well in advance of Christmas Eve so you have more than enough time to develop the wrapping for each gift thoughtfully.

A great big brass bell has been added to reflect the bell in the paper design of this gift, and whoever receives it will have it to hang on the door for seasons to come. It's tied with a gigantic red bow, the color of which picks up the red in the paper. A length of gold-beaded

Seasonal greens or flowers can be a supportive or more dominant element in a gift wrap. In this Christmas wrap, a sprig of greens has been used to simulate a tree branch and a golden angel tree ornament "hangs" on it. The elaborately textured ribbon is tied only in a simple bow so as not to overpower the lovely ornament, yet with its rich color and texture it stands up and enforces the traditional spirit of the gift wrap.

Made completely from scratch, our rose-covered cottage is a unique gift box spirited with humor and whimsy. The construction is less difficult than one might expect. It is simply a four-sided box with two peaked ends upon which the roof rests. Cover the charming box in fabric or paper and secure it with a great big satin bow. To open the gift, you simply open the roof. You can create house boxes in different sizes and bring a country feeling to their decoration by sponging or stenciling windows and doors onto the sides.

To construct a fabric-covered keepsake house box, you will need a 36-inch (1 meter) square of ¼-inch (⅜-centimeter) foam board (available at framing, crafts, and art-supply stores), an art knife (such as an X-acto), white glue, a medium stiff-bristled brush, pencil, ruler, and ½ yard (½ meter) of cotton fabric.

Foam board is easy to cut and provides a sturdy base for constructing this box. Perhaps the most critical factor in achieving "architectural" success is to measure accurately with a ruler. And, since your knife blade should be very sharp, always remember to lay down a piece of cardboard before cutting to shield your work surface.

Whether you construct, find, or buy a box, the fact is that with some ingenuity you can transform it into an everlasting keepsake for letters or papers, favorite photographs, or any other personal memorabilia.

To accomplish this, you'll need a box, some white glue, a paintbrush, sharp fabric scissors, and some ribbon. Follow the instructions for the Keepsake Wrap on page 10, covering your box with fabric, which is attached with a thin, even layer of white glue.

Give one keepsake box this year and another the next, keeping in mind the colors used from gift to gift, and soon some lucky person will have a remarkable collection of prized boxes, each reusable and a significant remembrance of your labors.

1. To make a basic house box, begin by measuring a 6-by-10-inch (15-by-25-centimeter) piece of foam board for the base. Cut it out using the following technique: place the ruler against the line to be cut, and draw the knife blade down along the edge of the ruler with a moderate amount of pressure. Repeat if necessary to cut all the way through .

2. Measure and cut out 2 more rectangles, 6¼-by-9½ inches (15½-by-23¾ centimeters) each, to form the unpeaked sides.

3. To form the peaked sides, measure and cut out 2 more rectangles, 6-by-10¼ inches (15-by-25½ centimeters) each.

4. To make the peaks, measure and mark 2 points along the edge of each long side of the rectangles, 4¼ inches (10½ centimeters) from the top. Then mark the center point of the top edge, and draw 2 straight lines connecting it to the points on the sides. Cut away the corners along the lines you have drawn. Repeat with the other 6-by-10¼-inch (15-by-25½-centimeter) rectangle.

5. To assemble, place the base piece flat upon the work surface. Brush a thin line of glue along the edge of 1 of the short sides. Then take 1 of the peaked ends and press its flat edge against the

line of glue so that the 2 pieces are at a 90° angle. Either hold in place by hand during the next step, or insert a straight pin to keep the walls steady.

6. Using the same method, glue 1 of the 6¼-by-9½-inch (15½-by-23¾-centimeter) pieces in place, next to the peaked side, forming a corner. Repeat the process until each side has been glued to the base and the adjoining sides.

7. Allow your project to dry for at least a half hour before continuing.

8. To make the roof, measure a piece of foam board 10-by-10 inches (25-by-25 centimeters) and cut it out. Score it lightly down the center line with your knife, making a slit that doesn't go all the way through. Bend the roof piece in half along the scored line, and determine how much it has to be bent to form the roof by fitting it gently on the base.

9. To cover the box with fabric, first make sure all glue is completely dry. Then cut a piece of fabric measuring 12-by-36 inches (⅓-by-1 meter).

10. To glue the fabric onto the house, begin by brushing an even coat of glue all over one of the peaked sides.

11. Place the fabric face-down on the work surface. With a ¼-inch (⅗-centimeter) margin of fabric at the edge, lay the peaked side down on the fabric, leaving a 1-inch (2½-centimeter) overhang of fabric on both the top and bottom edge of the foamcore. Smooth out all wrinkles.

12. Brush glue evenly on the next side of the house, and turn the house over on the fabric, so that the side with the glue is against it. Pull the fabric taut, and smooth out any wrinkles. Repeat the process with the third side.

13. Before you secure the last side, however, stretch the ¼-inch (⅗-centimeter) overlap from the beginning of the fabric around the corner to the uncovered side and glue it down.

14. Then fold the side edge under to make a "hem," and glue the last side down in the same manner as the other sides.

15. Fold the remaining inch (2½ centimeters) of fabric hanging from the bottom edge of the box underneath the box, slitting it diagonally at the corners if necessary to make the folding easier. Glue it down underneath the box.

16. Trim the excess fabric on the top edge within 1 inch (2½ centimeters) of the edge, fold it over the rim of the box, slitting it diagonally at the corners if necessary, and glue it to the inside of the box.

17. To cover the roof, measure and cut out a 13-by-13-inch (32½-by-32½-centimeter) square of fabric. Keeping the roof piece bent at the correct angle at all times, brush the roof piece with glue, center the fabric over it and press it down, smoothing out any wrinkles.

18. Fold over any excess fabric, and glue it to the underside of the roof.

19. To secure the roof to the base, simply tie them together with a colorful ribbon as shown in the photo.

The same techniques may be used with paper instead of fabric. One roll of standard gift wrapping paper is more than enough to cover a house box of the above proportions. If you use paper, it might be fun to tear scraps of a contrasting paper (see page 17) for windows, doors, flower boxes, and shrubs and glue them on.

This cheery yellow attaché, or a similiar carrying case, can be a wonderful gift wrap or the gift itself. It could be the perfect thing to enclose a present for the graduate, secretary, boss, or anyone else who has to lug a lot around. In any case, it is a good example of how to dress up a hard-to-wrap package. Tie it up with a really wide ribbon that corresponds to the case in scale, and don't forget to add a few ornaments, like the colorful pencils and address book. Always tie ornaments on with the ribbon; tape may mar the surface.

The simple beauty of this tin pig cutout fits well with the brown-paper-wrapped package. The sponged black checkerboard design creates just the right amount of decoration to echo the country feeling. Since the pig is a piece of folk art, it has been securely tied to the package with a double-wrapped length of black ribbon tied with a country-clean loop bow. Using black and brown as the two color elements allows the beauty and strength of the cut tin pig to remain the focus of the package.

For this package, you will need plain brown wrapping paper, double-faced tape, a clean kitchen sponge, black acrylic paint, a container to hold the paint, the tin pig decoration (available at crafts or antique stores), and a length of black satin ribbon.

1. Wrap the package in the brown paper, using the Basic Seamless Wrap (see page 8).

2. Using a sponge cut into a small rectangular shape, sponge paint a checkerboard pattern along two sides of the package, as shown in the photo. Follow the instructions for sponge painting on page 14, and take care to use as little paint as possible to keep it from soaking through the paper.

3. Tape the tie attached to the pig decoration to one side end of the package, and position the pig on the front of the package.

4. Tie the black ribbon in a simple two-looped bow around the short end of the package, as shown in the photo.

Everyone finds they have dinner invitations, picnics to attend, or parties that require them to bring along some food. If you are bringing a gift of food and wish to give it some personalization, you might cover the tops of canning jars with material and tie ribbons around them, or you might present some bread in a pretty basket or tray, surrounded by wild flowers. A gift of freshly baked cookies will look especially inviting if they are tied up in small packets of varicolored tissue paper and stacked prettily in a reusable wire basket of an unusual shape, like the one in the photo. This wrapping method also works well when giving several individual jars of jams, mustards, vinegars and oils, or perhaps a bunch of small kitchen gadgets.

1. Cut sheets of tissue paper of various colors about 6 inches (15 centimeters) square if wrapping cookies, bigger for jam jars, etc.

2. Place whatever you're wrapping in the center of the tissue paper square, and gather the sides of the paper up around it. Tie with lengths of contrasting ribbon, curled if desired (see instructions on page 24).

3. Place all your tissue paper bundles in the basket and you're ready to go!

If you don't keep a supply of materials on hand for emergency gifts, you may find yourself coming up short on paper or ribbon when you need to have a gift ready immediately. Being creative and determined helps in this situation. Don't despair. You can still create an interesting package with contrasting patterns and shapes. Simply tape together several different types of paper to make a sheet large enough to wrap your gift and then use the Basic Seamless Wrap (see page 8). As long as the different pieces don't clash, your wrapping will have all the character of an abstract painting, complete with wit and graphic charm. It can be decorated further by pasting on small scraps of contrasting paper, then tying it with a ribbon, if you have one. It will have just the right appeal for an enthusiast of high-tech decor.

SOURCES

BALLOON CITY, U.S.A.
P.O. Box 1445
Harrisburg, PA 17105-1445

FIBER CRAFT MATERIALS
Kirchen Brothers
P.O. Box 1016
Skokie, IL 60076

HALLMARK CARDS
25th and McGee
Kansas City, MO 64108

HURLEY PATENTEE MANOR
RD #7
P.O. Box 98A
Kingston, NY 12401

RIBBONS BY OFFRAY RIBBON COMPANY
C.M. Offray & Son, Inc.
Rt. 24
P.O. Box 601
Chester, NJ 07930-0601

RIBBON NARROW FIBER COMPANY, INC.
565 Windsor Drive
Secaucus, NJ 07094

THE STEPHEN LAWRENCE CO.
450 Commerce Road
Carlstadt, NJ 07072